First edition for the United States and Canada published
in 2010 by Barron's Educational Series, Inc.

First edition of *Everybody Matters*
First published in 2010 by Wayland, a division of Hachette Children's Books

All inquiries should be addressed to:
Barron's Educational Series, Inc.
250 Wireless Boulevard
Hauppauge, NY 11788
www.barronseduc.com

Library of Congress Control No.: 2010925445

ISBN-13: 978-0-7641-4517-9
ISBN-10: 0-7641-4517-7

Printed in China
9 8 7 6 5 4 3 2 1

Manufactured by: Shenzhen Wing King Tong Paper Products Co. Ltd., Shenzhen, Guangdong, China.
May 2010

Everyone Matters

A FIRST LOOK AT RESPECT FOR OTHERS

PAT THOMAS
ILLUSTRATED BY LESLEY HARKER

BARRON'S

You have probably heard people use the word "respect." But do you know what respect means?

Respect is a little word,
with a very big meaning.

Respect is a word we use to describe valuing the worth of other people as much as we value our own.

Respect has to do with equality.

When you respect someone you see them as your equal, as being just as good as you are.

When you think of someone in this way, you pay more attention to the ways in which you are alike...

...and don't worry too much about the ways in which you are different.

Most of the differences
between human beings
are ones we can see
with our eyes.

What makes us alike are the
things we feel in our hearts.

13

There are some types
of respect that we
all deserve,

like being treated fairly, not being called names
or shouted at...

...and not being made fun of because we are different.

And there are some types of respect that we have to earn
by doing things like keeping our promises, being loyal,
being polite, listening, and being honest with others.

The more you show respect to others by doing these things, the more they will respect you in return.

What about you?

Can you think of some ways you can show respect to others?
Are there other things like animals and plants that need
our respect as well?

Some people think they can force
others to respect them...

...and some think they deserve respect even when they
haven't done anything to earn it.

These people act like bullies, and
try to scare people into doing
what they tell them to do.

But being scared of someone isn't the
same as respecting them.

Because when you are scared you feel like the other person is bigger, or better, or more powerful than you.

Respect always makes you feel that you are as important as anyone else.

Showing respect doesn't mean never disagreeing.

Everyone is entitled to have their own feelings and opinions—even if they are different from yours.

If you respect someone, you try to understand why they think or believe something—even if you don't think or believe it yourself. They have an equal right to their opinion.

Sometimes you just have to agree to disagree!

What about you?

Can you think of some times when you didn't agree with someone?
Can you think of ways to show someone that you respect them
even if you disagree with their opinion?

Everybody wants respect, but not everybody knows how to show it.

We all have to practice showing respect every day—
even grown-ups...

...because the more you practice, the better you get at it.

And when we all try
to respect each other,
and treat each other
as equals...

26

...our homes and schools—and even our world—become happier places for us all to work and play and live together.

HOW TO USE THIS BOOK

Showing respect means valuing the worth of other people as much as you value your own. In this sense, showing respect is about equality—treating others how you want them to treat you.

Parents are a child's first teachers and role models. And showing respect for your child is probably the best way to begin. You can do this by using kind words, helping when you can, sharing, listening to what others have to say, being honest and truthful, thinking before you speak and act, practicing good manners, controlling your temper, thinking about the feelings of others, and applying the principles of fairness at home and at work.

Self-respect is an important form of respect, since once we respect ourselves, it is easier to respect others. Children who feel valued for who they are, and who have been helped to learn self-respect take care of themselves, their belongings, and their responsibilities in a conscientious way, will find it easier to respect others.

Likewise, help your child to know that respect is more than avoiding conflict. It means that people know how to talk to each other, appreciate each other's differences and have a basic willingness to cooperate and compromise. Let children know that sometimes the most respectful solution is to agree to disagree. Not all conflicts can be resolved. But that doesn't mean that we can't respect each other and live and work peacefully side by side.

In a multicultural society respect is crucial. There are many ways to teach appreciation of diversity. Encourage open discussions at home about the ways in which we are all different and the ways in which we are all the same. In modern society, we mix and match many aspects of other cultures, for instance in what we eat, how we dress, the music we listen to. (English in particular borrows words from many different languages.) Point these out to your children as examples of common ground with other cultures.

Schools are ideal places to help teach respect, tolerance of differences, and appreciation of diversity. Teachers can do this by encouraging different student relationships through frequent changes of seating patterns and by forming and re-forming cooperative work groups in which children from different backgrounds are placed in varying social and work situations get to know each other and learn to get along.

In class, talk about what respect means, but also what it doesn't mean. What kinds of things or actions could be considered disrespectful? Students might provide such responses as rudeness, racism, bullying, gossip, criticism, and insults.

To emphasize the point that different people have different likes and dislikes, teachers can invite children to share something—a food, an activity, a place, or anything else—they like very much. After everyone has shared, ask some of the students to identify things that other students like but they don't like as much. This discussion is a good way to show that people should treat one another respectfully in spite of their differences.

Have students work as a class or in small groups to brainstorm responses to the question, "What does 'respect' mean to me?" Or have the students work together to come up with a set of "golden rules" of respect for the classroom.

BOOKS TO READ

Respect: Dare to Care and Be Fair!
Ted O'Neal (Abbey Press, 2001)

Learning to Be a Good Friend: A Guidebook for Kids
Christine A. Adams (One Caring Place, 2004)

Standing Up to Peer Pressure: A Guide to Being True to You
Jim Aver (Abbey Press, 2003)

Treat Me Right!: Kids Talk About Respect
Nancy Loewen (Picture Window Books, 2005)

Is It Right to Fight?: A First Look at Anger
Pat Thomas (Barron's Educational Series, Inc., 2003)

Stop Picking on Me: A First Look at Bullying
Pat Thomas (Barron's Educational Series, Inc., 2000)

My Manners Matter: A First Look at Politeness
Pat Thomas (Barron's Educational Series, Inc., 2006)

RESOURCES FOR ADULTS

Respect! Exploring Children's Rights in the UK and Around the World
Save the Children (Save the Children, 2008)

Respect (Adventures from the Book of Virtues)
(Golden Books Publishing Company, 1998)

Hands Around the World: 365 Creative Ways to Build Cultural Awareness and Global Respect
Susan Milford (Williamson Publishing Co., 1992)